TeeCee's Arborfield Odes

An illustrated collection of verses relating to the life and times of and at the Arborfield Army Apprentices School

By Tony Church

TeeCee's Arborfield Odes
By Tony Church

Second Edition 2007 by Las Atalayas Publishing

Written and Compiled by Tony Church
Copyright © 2007 Tony Church

The moral rights of the author have been asserted. All rights reserved. No part of this publication may be reproduced, stored in a retrieval system or transmitted in any form or by any means, electronic, mechanical or otherwise without the written permission of the Publisher.

Typeset and Design by kenandglen.com

ISBN 978-0-9556753-2-4

Printed in England

Dedication

Between 1936 and 2004 some 50,000 young men and women started their Army careers as apprentice soldier tradesmen at the Army Apprentice training establishment at Arborfield in Berkshire.

This book is dedicated to all of them.

Contents

The Author	6
Introduction	11
A Day in the Life of a Jeep	12
Boys No More	14
Boots	17
The Drill Pig	19
Rodeo	21
Christmas	23
The Firework Factory	25
Reveille	27
Retreat	29
Lights Out	31
Our Fred	32
Old Boys - Old Soldiers	34
Numbers and Initials	37
My First Time	39
A Hot Iron	40
The RSM	43
Trade Training	47
Jankers	49
The Anuual Reunion	52
The ECE	54
More Boots	57
The School Bands	58
Nil Tempus Fugit?	60
Our Bill	62
The Rev Bev	65
The Reds	66
Heroes	69
Passing Out Parade	70
A Soldiers Tale	75
Regrets	77
The 66'ers	79
Discipline	81
Whither Boys Scool	83
The Enemy Within	87
The Glorious Past	89
A Soldiers Tale	91
The Final Parade	93

About the Author

Tony was born in Kingston-upon-Hull and evacuated to a farm on the Yorkshire Wolds to escape 'the blitz'. He was educated at Endyke Lane Secondary School, leaving in 1954 at the age of fifteen, to work as an apprentice at *Blackburn and General Aircraft*, making the *Blackburn Beverley* transport aircraft. He then left civilian life to join the Army Apprentices School, Arborfield, training as a General Fitter. While there, Tony joined the Pipe Band as a learner drummer, rising to Apprentice Drum Major in 1957. In 1958, he passed out into REME and was first posted to 14 Command Workshop, Ashford, Kent, where he passed his 2nd-class Trade Test. Then in 1959, he was posted to the Junior Leaders Regt RA, Hereford, before moving on to Bramcote, Nuneaton, when the unit was relocated.

In June 1960, Tony had an emergency posting to the Command Workshop at Dhekalia in Cyprus, working at the VDRI (Vehicle Depot Repair Increment) - NOT the Venereal Disease Research Institution, as some claimed! This was an outlying unit, located on the beach near the 'Key' Cinema, which employed eight REME personnel and forty to fifty Greek and Turkish Cypriots on vehicle repairs. His job was to read vehicle inspection reports, order parts and progress them from stores to job completion. At tea breaks, he would step through the barbed wire, have a 10-minute swim in the Med, then carry on working! Tony was occasionally called out on riot squads, but things were improving until, after independence in October, he was posted back to the UK, travelling back on the soon-to-be redundant troopship *'MV Dunera'*.

In November, Tony was posted to 4 Trg Btn RAOC, Deepcut, Surrey, where he maintained all sorts of weird and wonderful RAOC equipment - Oxygen and Acetylene producing plant, Mobile Laundry and Shower units, cobbling machines and a fleet of ninety or so vehicles. When he arrived, the REME unit consisted of a Major, three WOs, six NCOs and approximately forty men. Upon leaving, three years later, the same work was being done by one ASM, himself (now promoted to Corporal) and six civilians. National Service had been phased out over the intervening years and this was the birth of the new, modern Army.

Having been married for 18 months, he was posted to 13 Field Survey Squadron RE, at Fernhurst, Haslemere. It was a lovely posting, set amid fir trees in deepest Surrey, a unit of sixty or so surveyors, printers and allied trades. Unfortunately, upon arrival, the first question he was asked was, *"Are you coming to Aden with us in a month's time?"* – illusions shattered! So, in January 1961, Tony and his unit flew from Gatwick, *en route* to his new posting, at Falaise Lines, Little Aden. In March, the CO announced that Aden had ceased to be an active service area, but the next month all hell broke loose up in the Radfan, with the war finally ending in July.

The unit was working flat out to survey and supply maps to Commanders in the field; the survey troops were regularly ambushed and eventually had to enlist the support of the Royal Marines as escort. Tony was with the survey troops 'up country', riding 'Tail End Charlie', carrying out repairs to the unit's four Land Rovers and two Bedford RLs, as they negotiated soft sand, flooded wadis and big boulders. He lost count of the clutches he changed and broken springs he fixed – all in a temperature of well over 100°C. Eventually the war died down and June, his wife, joined him, living in a married quarter in Crater, opposite the local jail and Armed Police Barracks. One interesting aspect of this location was that, when a full moon appeared, the noise in the jail reached horrendous proportions. Upon enquiring of their 'dhobi wallah' (laundry boy), he remarked that this was 'Macnoon'. Tony was trying to figure out who this mythical Scotsman was, when it was explained to him that the jail was also the mental home and 'Macnoon' was allegedly Arabic for *'nutty as a fruitcake'*! Shortly after this, the terrorism began, with both soldiers and civilians being shot in the streets, so reluctantly he had to send his wife home. The following January, Tony's tour ended, and he returned to the REME Depot at Arborfield. As he was due for demob in April, and having one month's resettlement leave, he handed in his kit at the Depot and entered civilian life once again.

Before being posted to Aden, June and Tony had taken out a mortgage on a house in Kirk Hallam, near Ilkeston, Derbyshire, which at the time had not been built. Now they were able to move in immediately, which was just as well, as son Paul was born one week after their return. With a new baby and a mortgage, Tony worked shifts as a maintenance fitter for *British Celanese* in Derby, eventually returning to Wokingham, his wife's home town, in 1970 - by then the proud father of a baby girl, Michaela. After two years, working at the Fighting Vehicles Research and Development Establishment (FVRDE) on Chobham Common, he eventually became a forklift Field Service Engineer, then eventually moving into management, a career he pursued until retirement.

The couple now lives in Titchfield, near Fareham in Hampshire, where their bungalow looks down over the Solent and they enjoy a panoramic view from Portsmouth to Cowes. They also own a chalet on the Solent at the end of Southampton Water, giving a grandstand view of the ocean liners, yachts, and all the activity that this busy stretch of water contains. Tony started writing the odd piece of verse as a contribution to the Arborfield Old Boys' website. He finds that it helps relax him and, more importantly, keeps him out of mischief!

BOYS
aged 14 to 16
HERE'S YOUR CHANCE
for a grand life & a fine career

As soon as you are 15 YOU can be accepted for training at the fine Army Apprentice Schools from which the Regular Army picks its best (and most highly paid) Technicians and Tradesmen. All you have to do is pass a straightforward Entrance Examination. Get through this (and you *can*) and for three years you will enjoy all the amenities of a fine Public School. You will be well boarded, fed, clothed and cared for, entirely without cost to you or your parents, and you will actually be *paid* while you learn to handle modern tools and equipment with skill and precision. Your training over you will be ready to join one of the Army's crack Technical Corps with every chance of quick promotion to Warrant Officer and opportunities of reaching commissioned rank. Don't waste this chance. Get your application in quickly!

ASK YOUR FATHER OR MOTHER TO WRITE NOW
Entries for the next Examination must be in by 1st November.

The Commandant of your nearest Army Apprentices' School will send full details of the school and gladly arrange for you and your parents to visit it. Write to whichever of these addresses is nearest to you, or to the *War Office*, A.G. 10, London, or apply to any Army Recruiting Office.

Commandant, ARMY APPRENTICES' SCHOOL - Chepstow - Monmouthshire
Commandant, ARMY APPRENTICES' SCHOOL - Harrogate - Yorks.
Commandant, ARMY APPRENTICES' SCHOOL - Arborfield - Berkshire

Introduction

The training of young soldier tradesmen provided the British Army with a valuable source of manpower for 65 years. The system of centralised Technical Schools for boys started as far back as 1923. Prior to the outbreak of World War II, Artificers RA, Armourers RAOC and other tradesmen for technical corps were trained at Woolwich, Hilsea and Chepstow. Boys were taken directly from school and taught a trade in a manner similar to that seen in British industry throughout the 50', 60's and 70's. The major difference, of course, was that military apprentices were also trained as soldiers, so that they could take their proper place in those regiments or corps to which they would eventually be posted.

In 1939 with the British Expeditionary Force now in France there was still a shortage of specialist soldier-tradesmen however, so it was decided that three new Army Technical Schools would be built at Arborfield, Chatham and Jersey to produce tradesmen for the special needs of the RAOC, RE and RASC respectively.

The Army Apprentices School at Arborfield was originally designed to house and train up to 1,000 apprentices at a time. In the 1990's the originally buildings had been replaced with those of a more modern construction - but to many old boys they were far more inferior to the original wooden and corrugated iron accommodation spiders and other buildings.

In 2004 the Labour government in their wisdom decided that apprentice training at Arborfield would cease completely and so it was that on the 12th August 2004 the last batch of Arborfield Army Apprentices from more than 50,000 before them passed out from the College to move into mans service.

For those who started their Army careers as Apprentice Tradesmen Arborfield has always held a special place in their hearts. TeeCee's collection of amusing and sometimes poignant verses reflects much of the life and attitudes of many who spent their formative years there.

A Day in the Life of a Jeep

Reveille's blast assaults your ears, you stumble from your pit,
All thoughts of sleep are left behind, while laying out your kit.
You've got an hour to get it all lined up with time to spare,
Before the dreaded bugle call to muster on the square.

Down for breakfast, join the queue, then senior divs appear,
You're gypped again - the rotten swine! But keep mouth shut for fear
Of rough reprisals later on, it isn't worth a light,
Being a jeep's just not much fun and you know it isn't right.

But that's the way it's always been, you know your time will come,
When it's your turn to be real mean and they'll, in turn, play dumb.
Collect your greasy eggs and tea, you've got no time to eat,
Then time your exit to miss the "Plates !" and beat a swift retreat!

Back to the billet. Room jobs now, you're on 'bump centre deck.'
Mix Zebo with that orange wax, you mustn't miss a speck
Of dirt - you really break your back, to get that shine just right,
A pity though, it won't last long when the lads return tonight.

Time to get the clobber on, boxed denims, shirt and tie,
Jacket, get your beret straight, one inch above the eye,
Pull on your boots, check webbing's right "Five minutes before's" the rule.
Late on Parade? Not on your life! You learn FAST at this school!

Half an hour of square-bound joy then follows, what a bind!
The bellowing of soldier- boys, enough to blow your mind!
But wait ! The day has just begun, there's lots more yet to come,
Workshop training, followed by a long cross country run!

March to the workshops, grab your file, attack that lump of steel,
Scrape to and fro till blisters show, until the midday meal.
Get gypped again, but what the hell, you're too fed-up to care,
Back to your room, it's time to change for PT, don't despair.

Cross country runs are good for you, so say the PTI's.
But no good arguing with those chaps, so under leaden skies
You set off at a steady jog, and head down Hogwood Lane,
And sure enough, within a mile, it's pouring down with rain.

Returning, knackered, cold and wet, you stagger to your room,
Go to the shower, there to find no lights to pierce the gloom.
The water's cold, you just can't see to get yourself cleaned off,
It's all supposed to make you hard, but all you feel is rough.

And when at last the day is done, you crawl back to your pit,
Your will to live **just** lingers on, although you'd like to quit.
So ask yourself as night time falls, "Is Civvy Street so good?"
"Would I go back to Civvy pay?"

       "TOO BLOODY RIGHT I WOULD!"

Boys No More

The great adventure had begun,
We'd left our families, homes, and gone
Away into the great unknown
Apprehensive, feeling lost, alone
And wondering what the future held,
Our hopes, though high, fear undispelled.

Then suddenly, no time to think,
Life's one long round of work, eat, drink,
Sleep. Spit and polish rule our lives,
Yet slowly, imperceptibly arrives
The bonds of friendship, long to last,
Throughout the years, strong, steadfast.

Friendships forged by joy and pain,
Shared escapades of loss and gain,
Yes, truly, we were brothers all,
Stronger ties than blood recall
The mutual feelings that we shared,
And how we laughed and joked and cared.

We see them still, through memory's haze,
The bright, long, glorious, carefree days,
When youth enjoyed the summers long,
Erased, the hard times, strife and gone
The times when we felt low,
Just golden days in minds eye grow.

But time exacts its bitter toll,
And young men age, grow frail and fall
Prey to the ever rolling years,
Life's toil and pain, sadness, tears,
No more the boys of days long past,
Till finally life ebbs at last.

Yet though life's span has run its course,
We need feel no anger, fear, remorse,
But be privileged to have shared in part
The life of those who, from the start,
Had given friendship unreserved,
No better epitaph deserved!

So we were blessed, much more than most
To have that comradeship, though lost
In passing years our youth,
Those ties still bind and yet, in truth
They live on, young, as when first we met.
They don't grow old. We won't forget.

Boots

Boots are useful things you know,
They keep your feet warm in the snow,
And they also have the knack
Of stopping toenails turning black.
And wearing boots quite often tends
To stop feet fraying at the ends.

Yes, without boots we'd be so sad,
Our tootsies cold, and chilblains bad
Would definitely infest our feet,
We'd have to limp, and then retreat
Back to our beds to make them well,
A barefoot life would just be hell.

So, wearing boots is good for you,
Your feet will thank you if you do,
And all the hours that you have spent
Burning bumps off, just intent
To burnish toecaps to high sheen,
Can earn you praise and high esteem.

So spit and polish, elbow grease,
Applied with verve, will always please
The CO, or the CSM,
Who'll gaze at them and then proclaim
That you're the one whose boots are best,
Promotion's yours ! Yes, you've impressed!

The Drill Pig

He stands, and looks with great distaste at quivering Jeeps lined up, aghast
At what he sees. And casts his eyes toward the sky above, and sighs.
"Cor Blimey! Here we go again, attempt to turn boys into men?
I don't know why I bother - straight! This 'orrible lot are gonna hate
My guts before the day is done." And pace stick raised, begins to run

His hapless victims round and round. "Left Turn! Right Turn!" Until the sound
Of crunching boots has finally stilled his raging sadists soul, and filled
His heart with sated, savage joy, as he continues to destroy
Their individual self-esteem, AND MOULDS THEM TO A PERFECT TEAM

This is the Army's way, you see, of changing their thoughts drastically,
Each one had thought he was the best, superior to all the rest,
A cut above the common herd, but now he's realized, it's absurd.
It bonds his pals in common cause, to help, encourage, for he knows
That they will do the same for him when times are hard, and things look grim.

So spare a thought for Drill Pigs too, they do the things they have to do,
For long term good in soldiers lives, so every one, in his way strives
To keep the Army's good repute, enabling them to then recruit
More men and boys, who'll carry on tradition, that's so bravely won.

(Rodeo was an extra weekend drill – punishment for minor transgressions)

Rodeo

Saturday lunchtime, Oh what bliss! Flaked right out, but Oh, what's this?
You've been a naughty boy it seems, and far from play, you know it means
That you'll be out, upon the square, in best SD, in suns hot glare,
Drilling for an hour or so, while all your mates get set to go
Out on the town to paint it red, while you're just marking time instead.

So heave a sigh, put on brave face, and best SD, best boots and lace
Them up, put on that belt, more depressed you've never felt.
If only you'd got out of bed the other day, than, instead,
Turned over for some extra kip, and given the duty sarge some lip,
At which point, he invited you to join the Company Orders queue!

So now the time's come to parade, you steel yourself for the tirade
Of Orderly Sergeants raucous shouts, as, left turn, right turn, turn about,
You don't know if you're coming or going, just keep on blindly following
The guy in front, don't make mistakes, ignore the heat and the aches
Of ankles, knees, calves and toes, just do everything that he does.

And now, at last, the end is near, "Dismiss!" is all you want to hear,
The sweat is running in your eyes, and, with all the other guys,
You've had enough, crime never pays, you've seen the error of your ways,
No way will you do this again, for one small slip, an hour of pain.
It's a game for cowboys to be won, but for squaddies – Rodeo's no fun!

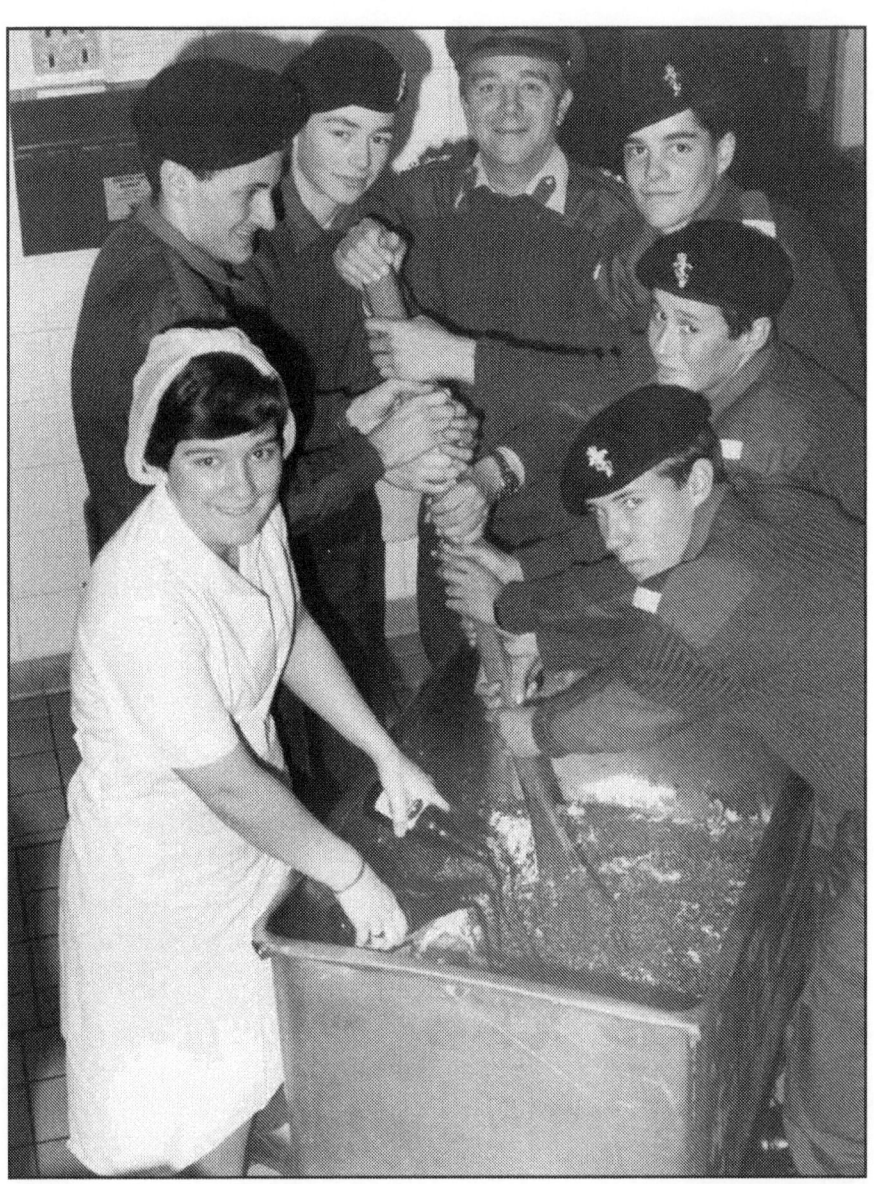

Christmas at Boys School (50's style)

I remember the Christmases at the old School,
High jinks and everyone playing the fool.
The dances, the parties, the air of relief
With the anticipation of going on Leave.
Concerts and comedy at the Camp Hall,
Hoisting "Drawers Dracula" up the flagpole.

The Bands in the Spiders, waking everyone up,
The CSM pouring "Gunfire" in your cup,
As you climbed from your pit, getting ready for home.
Collecting your Credits (White Fivers for some!)
Then down to the Camp Hall to hear the CO
Wishing all 'Festive Greetings' – but we're itching to go
And get changed into civvies, to spend all our Loot
On our nearest and dearest – and then get hotfoot

Down to the Station, get on the train
To take us to freedom, away from the pain
Of study and foot drill, away from the Bull,
Two weeks of bliss, living life to the full.
Yes, Christmas at Boys' School never was dull,
(Come to think of it, "Dull" never happened at all!)

So I'll live with my memories of the Yuletide,
And raise a glass to us 'Saga Louts', brimming with Pride!!

The Firework Factory

In a back lane in Arborfield, long, long ago,
Stood a firework factory, right in the shadow
Of an Army Apprentices place, which was known,
As a finishing school of worldwide renown.

Now this factory was mostly hidden by trees,
And the boys took no notice, too busy to see
What went on at the works, in fact they bored,
There were things more important than what they had stored.

And, of course, they stored cordite, gunpowder and stuff,
Without it, the bangers would scarcely go, "Puff !"
And rockets would hardly be able to fly,
Roman Candles just wouldn't get into the sky.

So life was quite peaceful, with nothing much on,
When all of a sudden, a detonation,
Rocked the Spiders, the Cookhouse, the classrooms et al,
And a column of smoke covered all in its pall.

Not waiting for orders, some lads jumped the fence,
And twenty or so headed into the dense
Conflagration, the noise, the smoke and the heat,
Rolling out drums, though they hardly could breathe.

And when it was ended, the following day,
The National Press had this much to say:
"Boys from the neighbouring school were so brave,
Rolling out drums of gunpowder, to save
The lives of the workers, and in the end, won,
Everyone owes them, a heartfelt 'Well Done'!"

The lads were nonplussed on hearing this news,
They'd reacted as trained, "Nothing special" they mused,
Though one of them was heard to say to his chums,
"Bloody Hell! So THAT's what was inside those drums!"

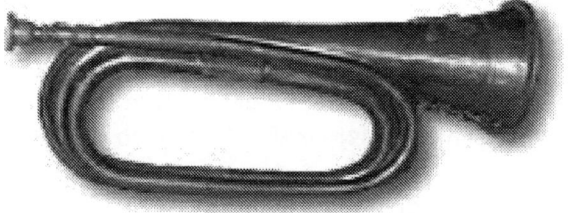

Reveille

Sweet Dreams. You lie, warm, far away
From toil and turmoil, a world so grey.
Wrapped in slumber, on sleep's wings
Your mind divorced from worldly things.

Then faint sound, breaking through the veil,
And growing louder, urgent, hails
The consciousness awake, to hear
The bugle calling, loud and clear.

Then, with a crash, the door swings wide,
A shadowy figure looks inside,
And flicks the switch, lights come alive,
The Orderly Sgt has arrived!

He murmurs greetings, asks so nice,
If we slept well, and, would a slice
Of toast be wanted with the tea
He's brought in so considerately?

Like Hell he does! He clatters in,
Bangs the lockers - what a din!
"Off Cocks, On Socks!" you hear the cry,
You won't sleep now, don't even try!

So put your feet down on the floor,
Get washing kit, head for the door
Down for a shave, ignore the pain,
Another day is here again!

Provost Sgt Fred Silver with his Buglers

Retreat

The lengthening shadows stretch over the Square,
    shading the fast fading sun,
Figures stroll leisurely in the half-light,
    work for the day now is done.
Muted voices, occasional laughs,
    as they quietly walk on their way
to return to their rooms from the evening meal,
    to relax at the end of the day.

A solitary figure appears in full dress, and marches to stand,
    centre Square,
Then places the bugle, slung from his shoulder, to his lips,
    breathing in the cool air,
The first tones ring out,
    the echoes return with descending notes cascading by,
And all who are present, pause and then stop,
    and snap to attention, heads high.

The flag on the flagstaff then slowly descends,
    while the bugle continues to play,
And hands on the corners fold with great care,
    as the long, plaintive notes fade away.
The tableau comes back to life, figures are moving,
    only still shadows remain,
The spell is now broken. Retreat has been sounded.
    Tradition is safe, yet again.

Lights Out

The bustling vigour of the day fades in a calm, reflective way
To thoughts of restful, quiet things. Conclusion of that time now brings
The nightly veil to cover all, in cool dark blackness, then the call
Is heard - low, softly, urgent, clear, inviting everyone who hear
Its message, as nights shades creep into the world. It's time to sleep.

Notes hang, suspended, on the air. Echoes seek the shadows there,
The studded stars, the moon so bright, contrasting the dark of night.
Another day draws to its close, the busy scene turns to repose
As muffled calls from rooms around, fade away, until the sounds
Are finally quieted, all is still, until the dawn, a sweet idyll.

Our Fred

He was five feet three in his socks, I suppose,
With a small black moustache just under his nose,
Three chevrons affixed to his upper sleeve,
With a red and black armband, lead one to perceive
That this was the guardian of the main gate,
The one to avoid, if getting in late
From a night on the town, or just slightly drunk,
If he was on duty you knew you were sunk.

No drainpipe trousers passed his eagle eye,
Without remonstration, and if one were to try
To argue that these were okay, try to fool
This veteran soldier, out came the rule,
Then the cry, "Fifteen inches!" assaulted your ears,
And you knew it was hopeless, for over the years
He'd honed to perfection all of the ploys
That had been tried on, by hundreds of boys.

This wily old soldier ran a guesthouse,
Full board and lodging, and certain to rouse
The guests from their slumbers, at no extra cost,
Provided that they actively humoured their host
By helping with housework, and some minor chores,
With verbal encouragement, in shape of roars
Of derision, to turn the air blue,
Till all within sparkled, and glistened like new.

Maestro of the fire pump, he tried to show those
Who were on fire picquet the right way to hose
Down an inferno, and be able to get
Personnel out of danger, but he often got wet
Due to some inexperienced, ham fisted Jeep
Who'd pull the wrong handle, or fail to keep
To his detailed instruction, so in the end that,
He'd vent his frustration and jump on his hat!

His immaculate garden was his pride and joy,
But weeding and digging would always annoy
His guests, who, in fits of bad temper ensured
That seeds, when grown up, spelt out words that were rude!
When his sole means of transport, his trusty old bike,
Needing refurbishing, he sought to strike
A bargain with one guest, who, armed with paint pot,
Painted frame, tyres and saddle – the whole blooming lot!

He wasn't amused, I think it's fair to say,
And his invective, impressive, was heard far away,
As the guest, with demeanour so innocent then,
Saw that his sense of humour had somehow worn thin,
So in self preservation, seeing thunderous frown,
He legged it quite smartly till things had calmed down!
But our hero found out that he hadn't impressed,
When he found that he'd do extra time as a guest!

He was certainly not the most popular chap,
His duties precluded him being just that,
Though for ten years he jealously guarded that gate,
Fulfilling his duties, ignoring the hate
And resentment that always accompanied his task.
Never to have the occasion to bask
In the warm glow of friendship of lads in his charge
He'll not be forgotten, our Rifle Corps Sarge!

Old Boys – Old Soldiers

Their hair is greyer, growing thin, the eyes less keen, waists less trim,
Yet in their hearts they're still sixteen, young now, as they'd ever been.
Though time creeps on, on silent feet, the memories, so bittersweet,
Come flooding back to fond recall, when once again they meet, and all
The years evaporate, they're in their prime once more with mates
Whose nicknames, given, when so young, appear as though they'd never gone.

The easy comfort that they feel when with old friends, returns to seal
Them in a personal, private state, which no one could appreciate,
Unless, like them, they'd shared their life - the good, the bad, the joy, the strife.
They slip back into ways of speech. Words, long forgotten oft-time, reach

Into the brains subconsciousness, igniting memories in the quest
To bring to mind events long gone, when days were sunny, summers long.

The camaraderie warms the heart, captures time when at the start
Of their careers, when fresh and young, all to gain, on the first rung
Of life's long ladder, climbing up, try to achieve to gain the top
Of their profession, strong and bold, success was there, to have and hold.
But older now, and wiser too, they reminisce and think of who
Had started with them, now long gone, and count those left to carry on.

But lessons learned so long ago, which shaped their lives and helped them grow
Into the men they are today, have helped them travel life's highway
And meet the challenges it brings, to overcome the many things
That might bring lesser persons down, unfortunate that they'd not grown
In youthful company of their peers, during those important years
Of laughs and jokes, eventful days, influenced in so many ways.

At first it seems at casual glance that it's old sweats recalling once
Again their soldiering days gone by, yet there is more than meets the eye
To this. They think of times now gone, when promises, relied upon
Would be kept, the consciousness of folk in general still was less
Directed to material things, truth and honour which then brings
Our lives into a higher plane - virtues we won't see again.

The hectic pace of life lived now, the onward rush to gain somehow
At cost of conscience, wealth and fame, no motive now to 'play the game',
Just blunder on, ignore the rest, the selfishness, will now attest
That values Old Boys learned are dead, and greed, self interest, rule instead.
That's why they prize these moments, when they turn back time to live again
In the gentler, honest age they knew, among those friends so good and true.

Numbers and Initials

The very first thing we had to remember
When taking the shilling, was our Army number.
On pain of reprisals too awful to bear,
We had to recite it, like learning a prayer.

Without numbers, the Army would cease to exist,
There are millions of them, too long here to list.
They cover all aspects of military life,
We encountered them daily, yes, numbers were rife.

Two-Five-Two was the one to make you feel blue,
And coupled with letters, DRO's One and Two.
And what about Army Form FMT3 ?
When you've just bent the end of your new TCV.

And, beloved of REME, the Ten-Forty- Five,
Plus the Ten-Forty-Three, (first-class licence to skive!)
Your life was mapped out on AB 64
Part One and Part Two, these you couldn't ignore.

For without them, you didn't stand much of a chance
Of receiving your pay, so they were, on balance
A real advantage and something to treasure,
One of few forms you could cherish with pleasure.

These are examples of what we endured,
Like AWOL, this struck if you went overboard,
Or not even that, if you ran out of time,
By failure to make Twenty-Three-Fifty-Nine !

Yet GOC's, C-in-C's, CREME's and such,
To civilians, they might as well be double Dutch,
But to squaddies, well versed in this strange, shorthand speak.
It saves explanation and preserves the mystique !

?

MY FIRST TIME

A word to preface this ode,
Don't lick your lips and leer,
It isn't what you think it is,
I'd like to make it clear
That actually, it's fictional -
Don't like to disappoint,
So stick your eyes back in your head,
Read on - you'll get the point!

You were the first. I will confess, now years have come and gone.
And looking back through mists of time, the memory's still strong,
Of how I'd lie awake at dawn, knowing you'd be there,
To wake me with your dulcet tones, showing how you cared.
And, sometimes, you'd give me a dig to rouse me from my sleep,
Murmuring sweetly in my ear, as from my bed you'd creep.

I was your slave. You knew that too, you just could do no wrong,
I'd hang upon your every word, to me a joyful song
Of loving and devotion. Reminding me of songbird's trill,
At your command I'd gladly go and shovel bits uphill.
And yes, in life, as we all know, a little rain must fall,
Yet even in our monsoon days, I'd still obey your call.

Even when I made you shout, you didn't really mean it,
And if you thought that something was too dirty, I would clean it.
For I could see that secretly you liked to look ferocious,
But really, it was all an act, you always were precocious!
You'd sometimes criticize the way I dressed, so I would go
And change into something you'd like, I loved to please you so.

I'd have my hair styled, just a bit, to gain your fond approval,
Even if you insisted on complete, total removal.
Yes, I was putty in your hands, to mould as you saw fit,
And no word of complaint from me ever passed my lips.
So there. Now, after all this time it's out, but I will wager,
You didn't guess it was addressed to my first Sergeant Major !!

A Hot Iron, Brown Paper and a Shaving Brush

Of three years training constantly to learn a trade, efficiently,
And military training simultaneously, I reckon, in the end, that we
Spent in all, (industriously) at least nine months, toiling endlessly
To clean our kit and rooms, to be inspected so officiously
By those told by the powers-that-be, to watch our conduct carefully.

So expertise with iron and brush, with Bumpers there to pull and push
Across the floor, till all shone bright, no speck of dirt shown up to blight
The pristine palace that we made, to put the others in the shade,
And earn ourselves the plaudits loud, of NCO's to make us proud
Of all our efforts to excel, by months of practice, done so well.

The bucket, once so grey and dull, polished bright, reflecting all
The sunbeams chased through windows clean, and the lockers in between
Shining like the the midday sun, aligned precisely, one by one.
Alongside beds and bed blocks smart, guaranteed to lift the heart
Of all who'd slaved to make it so, a truly grand, illustrious show.

And, as we stand there,dressed to kill, knife-edge creases,sharper still
Than well honed blades, with belts so white, and boots with toecaps shining bright
Gleaming buttons, all arrayed in perfect order, on parade.
Who would guess the stress and strain that we went through to finally gain
This spectacle of orderliness, immaculate in kit and dress?

The previous night, in midst of chaos, scenes of unbelievable pathos,
As twenty anxious, sweaty Jeeps, enough to make a grown man weep,
Queued up to press their best SD with just one iron, and desperately,
Impatiently, to get it done, insulting, barracking the one
Who, with brown paper, water, brush, endeavoured to placate the crush.

The smell of scorching filled the air, steam and swearing, moans and glares
As tramline creases came to light, so, cursing, tried to put it right.
And in the panic, big brown burn, with silver coin attempt to turn
It back into its normal hue, rubbbing down the marks anew,
Then giving it a final press with paper brown, at last - success !

Yet, come the dawn, inspection time, those scenes have faded from the mind,
Everything is calm, and yet, this time next week you'll safely bet
That it'll be the same again - controlled panic - and it's plain
For all to see, no matter how you try to organize it, still, somehow
It always ends up - you can guess - a muddled, never ending mess !!

RSM N T Osborne PWRR

The RSM

He strides, like God, upon the Square, there's apprehension in the air.
An awesome figure, carved in stone, he stands erect, aloof, alone.
The eagle eye surveys the scene, nostrils flare, and from between
His lips comes forth a strident roar. Hundreds flinch, and then, before
The next executive command, they, in expectation stand
Anticipating the loud blast, to propel them into fast
Reaction, and the moment when the expletive explodes again
Into their ears, they'll act as one, boots raise the dust – parade's begun!

With pace stick swirling to and fro, he marches them round, fast and slow.
Berating all who fail to match his standards, or, not up to scratch
With drill or dress, they'll pay the price, and in the future will think twice
Before they carelessly perform and face his wrath, endure the storm
Of his displeasure, loud and clear, extremely painful to the ear!
Yes, he's the Master of the Square and woe betide all those who dare
To desecrate the sacred ground, by slouching or playing around.
They'll find they're sweeping it all day, as punishment fits the crime, they say,
And learn the lesson taught to them - you don't mess with the RSM!

Fitting and Turning

Trade Training

We joined the army as young boys, our aim, to learn a trade,
So, in the very early months, a foundation was laid
To make us useful with our hands, and learn to use the tools,
Gain expertise in basic skills, and learn about the rules
Of engineering theory, how to make ourselves proficient
At filing, sawing, blacksmithing, in short, to be efficient
So that, after our apprenticeship, as members of the Corps
We'd keep the reputation of the school, as always, to the fore.

To this end we toiled, perspired, to gain the skills we sought,
Endless chipping, filing lumps of metal, we were taught
That when, "up at the sharp end" no machines would be around,
These basic skills, acquired today, invaluable, would astound
And win the admiration of those relying on
Our expertise and aptitude for improvisation.
For basic skills such as we learned, could make the difference
Between success's great reward, or failure's consequence.

The blisters, cuts and bruises, the burns that we sustained,
Were marks of honour, borne with pride as manual skills we gained.
Whether in the blacksmith's shop, amidst the hot emissions,
Sweating, trying hard to beat hot steel into submission.
Amidst the smoke, the heat, and through the overpowering noise,
The hammers swung and anvils rung by keen and eager boys.
Or in the fitting shops where trade test work, so intricate,
Was laboured over in the quest to make it accurate.

At the end of workshop training, final tests had to be faced,
To show we'd mastered all the skills, and swiftly, as we raced
To beat the deadlines that our shrewd instructors had devised,
We filed and polished our test pieces, cunningly disguised
The odd faux pas - hoped to escape the ever seeing eye
Of the dreaded test inspector – it was always worth a try!
But futile, he'd seen all the tricks and wheezes they'd employed
O'er all the years, by thousands of young, devious, cunning boys.

Now, looking back through time, and with the knowledge that it brings,
We see, and can appreciate the very many things
That we were taught so thoroughly, with no expense in mind,
And quality the yardstick that applied, back at that time.
No time was wasted; we worked hard, instructors worked hard too,
Their dedication to their work, ensuring that those, who
Deserved success, should gain the goals which in the future lay.
We owe our heartfelt thanks to them, for showing us the way.

Jankers

A/T O'Toole had been such a fool, going out when he should have been in.
So the very next day, with no undue delay, he was marched in to explain his sin.
The CO said, "O' Toole, while you're at this school, Standing Orders you have to obey."
"And to help you reform, seven days you'll perform, and confined to these barracks you'll stay."

O'Toole was so sad, it was hard for the lad to watch all his mates go to town,
While he had to work - he felt a right berk – peeling spuds till his fingers wore down.
And not only that, he had also to start getting kit bulled for evening parade,
Best SD to press, boots, belt, and then dress, attention to detail was paid.

For he knew, if he failed, he would then be assailed by the Orderly Sergeants great wrath,
And the following day, the price he would pay, on another charge, and that is tough.
For the cycle'd begin, the chances to sin while on Jankers, they would multiply,
So a seven day stint could become in an inst't, a fortnight or worse, could apply.

Therefore, duly at nine, he stands in the line of Defaulters, so nervous and glum,
While the Sergeant, so slow, inspects the first row, as he's waiting for his turn to come.
The Sarge, with a frown, eyes him up and then down, and turns on his heel, walks away.
Then O'Toole grits his teeth, breathes a sigh of relief, he's survived for yet one more day.

/ continued

The following dawn, O'Toole was forlorn at the prospect of six days to do,
All that bulling and beezing, a prospect displeasing, at the thought, his despondency grew.
So, up at Reveille, his courage he rallied, for he had an appointment with Fred,
And if he was late, such a terrible fate of more days, which filled him with dread.

Then, down to parade, with the others, he made his weary way to the Guardroom,
What jobs would he do? The Cookhouse, he knew, would be spuds again, peeling till noon.
But he thought he'd got lucky, a job not so mucky, he pulled QM's detail – that's good!
Inside, in the warm and the dry, he would try to filch items of kit if he could.

With his loot in his pocket, he knew he could flog it, when back to the Spider he went,
Selling ill-gotten gains, he would then take great pains to profit from his punishment.
But alas and alack, when reporting back to the QM's department, he found
That instead of work cushy, with whitewash and brush, he was shown a dirty great mound

Of coal in the yard, and the going was hard, but "coal has to be whitewashed", it states,
To stop boys thieving the coal, then heaving it all, over the fence, to their mates.
Who, back at the Spider, then sat down beside the stove, stoking away till it glowed.
But the coal that was nicked, left a black mark, when picked, and the crime then quite obviously showed!

So O'Toole learned a lesson, it's no use just guessing that jobs can be doddles, no fear!
To make such assumption shows sheer lack of gumption, as he found, while whitewashing the gear.
He thought that he'd cracked it, when he attracted the QM job, and so he laughed,
Forgetting that QM's activities ranged wide, from cushy, to downright hard graft!

The worst time he'd spend was at the weekend, the Saturday film in Camp Hall,
While he polished the brass and mowed all the grass, he could hear the lads having a ball.
And so, as the days of his time slipped away, as he tried to avoid further strife,
Released at the end, he vowed not to offend ever again in his life !

And so it goes on, Jankers never was fun, it's a punishment one must avoid,
But to give it wide berth, it never is worth to get those placed above you, annoyed.
Or you'll live to regret it, and they won't forget it, so humour them, make them feel good
So creep if you have to, although you won't want to, it's better than peeling those spuds!

The Annual Reunion

They journeyed back from far and near,
   to swing the lamp again,
Wearing out their hobnailed boots,
   as they marched down Memory Lane.
The Old Boys gather once a year to celebrate their past,
They drink a toast, good health,
   and cheer their friendships, holding fast.
They march, heads high, the medals glint and years just fall away,
As once again they stand in line, as true as yesterday.

Then, in silence, gathered round the solitary gates,
The garden by the hallowed ground,
   where the ghost of Fred still waits,
Remembering comrades, the times they shared,
   whose final posting came,
And now stand watch on Heavenly Guard,
   to muster once again.
Onward then, to celebrate the golden boys now here,
The toasts and speeches dedicate their fifty glorious years.
And afterwards, well fed, content,
   the same old questions rise,
"Who was that guy? Know where he went ?"
   The laughs, the jokes - the sighs.

And so they all prepare once more,
   to go their separate ways,
Old bonds renewed, strong to endure,
   goodwill that never strays.
The buildings now are long, long gone, a history mark in time,
But the spirit of the boys lives on, in men now in their prime.
They keep it fresh, each year renew that special feeling when,
In twelve months time they'll all return, to do it once again,
and again and again!

The ECE

The lad, who as an ECE trains, is credited with superior brains,
Because his diagnostic skills require him sometimes to fulfil
A knotty task that's sight unseen, where theory counts, a mind that's keen
And razor sharp, so he can tell where problems lie, and almost smell
A faulty loom, or diode, duff, armed with his wiring diagram rough,
He squints at multi-coloured wires, stays on the job and never tires,
Until success has been secured, discomfort, tiredness, all endured
To keep the ECE's, in their grace, on Gods Right Hand - their rightful place!

But as an afterthought, be fair, VM's must all deserve their share
Of credit. And the allied trades, whose skill and muscle also made
The REME what it is today, the finest force, far and away,
So all you tradesmen, take a bow, you made the Corps what it is now!

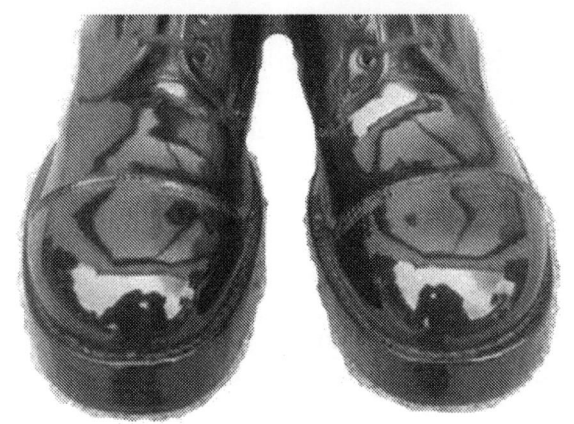

More Boots - A story with a moral

A/T Snodgrass had a plan, that with bulled boots he'd be stickman.
When mounting guard, he'd show the rest how smart he was, and with well pressed
Trousers he'd be sure to score, while others stagged, he could snore
At leisure in his comfy bed - let others stand on guard instead.

So, with his new boots in his hand, and red hot handled spoon as planned,
He laboured long into the night, burned and polished, till first light
Saw Snoddy's boots, a work of art, a sight to lift a Sergeant's heart.
The glossy sheen like ebony shone and, in his heart, he knew he'd won.

When time came for the guard to mount, our Snoddy tried, on no account
To let his shiny boots be marred by accidental kicks, and hard
As others really tried, as stickman then, he would preside.
For this was his big moment, when his labours wouldn't be in vain.

"Guard, Shun!" The order rang out loud and Snoddy, keen and oh, so proud,
Picked up his left foot, slammed it down, but as the sole bit in the ground,
The toecap, gleaming, flew away, and much to Snoddy's great dismay,
Exposed a big toe, shining bright, through rotten sock. Oh, what a sight!

So Snoddy's plan all came to nought, but could have worked, if he had thought
When, spoon in hand, he'd made a point of missing stitches at the joint
Where toecap meets the upper part, he wouldn't finish in the cart.
All of which just shows, I guess, that graft don't always mean success!

The School Bands

The lilt of music fills the air, the Boys' School bands are on the Square!
Rhythms dancing on the breeze, as marching feet stretch out to seize
And hold the beat in four-four time, while horns and trumpets, drums and chimes
Breathe life into the weary soul, raising spirits - that's their role,
To give that music added pep and put spring into weary step.

Then, marching paused – inspection time – the skirl of pipes begins to climb
In slow, such slow, close harmony, the plaintive airs and melody
Rise over the assembled throng, soothing sounds that cause the songbirds
To cease their trills and hesitate, to compete with such a thrilling, great
Uplifting sound that evokes in men, visions of a Scottish glen.

And, stepping off, they all combine to give a rousing, roaring, fine
Rendition of a well known air, as playing, marching with great flair,
They pass the dais, straight as a die. Drum Majors, maces held on high
Salute - eyes right - and then proceed along the square to finally lead
Them off parade, their task complete. Now all that's heard is tramping feet.

But versatility is the norm and the Military band is quite at home,
Playing dances, jazz, palm court, or tuneful sounds of any sort.
At functions grand or venues small, they'll persevere and give their all
In pursuit of the excellence that marks their sheer accomplishment.
They give the School good value too, their efforts great, achievements true.

The Pipe band also gets around, at village fetes they're often found,
And carnivals at summertide, but on Burns Night they hit their stride.
With Haggis Pipings to attend, demand's so great, to avoid offence
They move around at double speed, toasting Rabbie, then they need
To move on to the next venue – another toast, or one, or two!

This really tends to slow them down, but not for shirking they're renowned,
They carry on so manfully that even if there's two or three
More places they must go to play before the finish of the day,
They'll valiantly consume the tot, then play until they've done the lot,
Then totter back to their cold beds and on the morrow, nurse their heads!

But both the bands are at their best, on ceremonials that attest
To skills they learned while at the School, of discipline, and keeping cool
At all times under pressure, so they'll play until it's time to go.
As "Sunset"s last notes die away, remember these boys as they play,
These are not full time careers – it's just their hobby – for three years!

Nil Tempus Fugit?

In memory of the Naafi Break

Are we as happy, more content,
Than years ago, when it just meant
We lived our lives as best we could?
Respected all and firmly stood
Up for our freedom, made the choice
Of what we did, without the voice
Of interfering people, who
Would tell us what to say and do?

If we could change the present race
Of life, we should reduce the pace,
And pause awhile, take stock again,
Wind back the clock to those days when
We savoured life's more leisurely flow,
Appreciating time to go
More slowly on our chosen way,
Less stress, more fun, more time to play.

Consider how we used to work,
Full effort made, we did not shirk,
But still took time from labours too,
No rat-race then, though lots to do.
We took the breaks, refreshed our mind,
Then, rested, went back to the grind,
So when the daily work was done,
With conscience clear, we'd then have fun.

Though at the present time, it seems
That pressure is the only means
To motivate all those who toil,
No time for leisure, lest it spoil
The targets set by those who judge.
And consequently it's a drudge,
No satisfaction to be gained,
Just heartache, headache, ulcers, pain.

How different, therefore, would it be,
If those in charge set workers free
To enjoy life, give them their chance,
Encourage independent stance.
To let free thinking make the pace
Would make our world a better place,
So turn back time, as once was said,
"Let's all relax, you're a long time dead!"

OUR BILL

He's a quiet, unassuming gent,
Which does belie his deep intent
To keep the Old Boys to the fore,
In his dealings with the Corps.
The work he does behind the scenes
On our behalf quite often means
He burns the candle at both ends,
No quitter he, much time he spends
Cajoling, charming those on high
In his quest to satisfy
The needs of members and their kin,
And usually, he gets to win.
With his staunch allies, Keith and Fred,
An awesome team, it must be said,
They tackle problems day by day,
And usually they find a way
To succeed satisfactorily,
Employing great diplomacy.
Yes, they're the ones to make it work,
Never were they ones to shirk !

When Bill was younger, just a boy,
He'd wear the shades and then employ
His comb through dark and bushy thatch
Until he was a perfect match
For Orbison - that's right - " Big O " !
Which really pleased him even though
'Tis said the singer had his fill
Of folk confusing him with Bill !
Alas, the years did take their toll,
The hirsute one then saw it fall
And disappear, although, no doubt,
The Old Boys made him pull it out
In sheer frustration now and then,
Facing problems yet again.
His part-time (!) job at the museum,
(He hides in there where they can't see'im),
Means he's always on the ball,
And though he isn't very tall,
If dedication's stature's test,
Our Bill will tower o'er all the rest !!

THE REV BEV

Written on the occasion of his 58th Birthday

It came to pass, the Lord spake unto one young fresh faced youth.
"Go forth and spread the Word, the entire message and the truth
Of Christian Faith, reclaim the sinner's souls." And it was so,
The youth, responding to the call then knew that he must go
Among the people, even though, while in the military,
He knew that it would not be done so very easily.

And Lo, as was commanded, the righteous path he trod,
Till, when done with soldiering, he gave his life to God.
Not for him the pleasures of licentious soldiery,
He put aside those wordly things and joined the Ministry,
Where, to this day, he practises all that The Lord ordained,
Dispensing comfort and good cheer, Gods mysteries explained.

"Who is this saint in human guise?" We hear the plaintive cry.
"This servant of all Godly things, this reverential guy?"
The answer is quite easily found if down to Wales you go,
It's Bev the Rev, our Birthday Boy! Good on you, Boyyo!!
One problem though, you have no chance to keep your age concealed,
Your Intake broadcasts to the world when you joined Arborfield!!

"THE REDS"

This song used to be sung in the back of trucks going to and from manoeuvres and on many occasions when the would gather together on some of the less formal occasions such as the Company or Christmas dinners. It is now sung regularly and raucously at Old Boy Reunions.

"Cheers, Cheers the REDS are here,
What the hell do we care?
What the hell do we care?

Cheers, Cheers the REDS are here,
Why the hell do we care now?

For it's a grand old school to fight for,
For its a grand old song to sing.

When you hear its history,
It's enough to make your heart feel GLAD

We don't care what Chepstow says
As on our way we go,

For we only know
that there's goner be a show
and the RED supporters will be there

They're at the NAAFI
queuing up for buckshee tea,
(without the sugar)
queuing up for buckshee TEA!"

Sir Arthur Sullivan composed the tune and Gilbert the vocal score,
But the Arborfield lads didn't much like the words,so decided to invent a few more.
And that was the birth of the school battle hymn,(although no-one really knows when,)
Which was captured by a thousand young voices time and time over again.

It rang across the school playing fields and resounded around the Camp Hall,
And visiting teams came to fear the sound as a harbinger of their downfall.
Many a boxer hanging over the ropes really thought that his last hour had come,
Till, faint, far away, through the mist of the pain came the strains of that inspiring song.

Like a shot of adrenaline via his heart, it exploded straight into his brain,
Then, revitalized, he bent to his task to the ever-repeated refrain.
With the sound in his ears of exuberant cheers, he pounded and punched with aplomb,
Till the poor adversary, who had thought he was winning, soon found out that something was wrong.

For he then realized that he wasn't just facing one person alone in the ring,
And, at first undaunted, he found himself haunted by THE tune they started to sing.
So, love it or not, "The Reds" holds a slot in most Old Boys long standing affection,
For it marked at that time the team spirit sublime that's remembered in fond recollection.

But as years rolled along, the strains of the song faded into the past, now long gone,
And the voices, so youthful which sang it so tuneful are now just a low baritone.
'Cos the lads who remembered it now are quite aged, and feeling a tiny bit sad,
For that song represented our youth and recalled the great unity, once, that we had.

HEROES (?)

Heroes. Do they deserve the name? Was it for glory that they came
To serve their country? "No!" They'd say, t'was for the prospect to obey
And answer to their nations need for fine young folk to take the lead
In causes just. Defend the weak, wherever tyrants try to seek
To force their will upon all those who yearn for freedom from their cause.

But call them heroes? They would call it journalistic hyperbole.
Just soldiers, trying to bring peace to all who suffer. Work to cease
Their misery, make life again a worthwhile thing, and free from pain
Of prejudice, an end to strife. Return Gods given gift of life
That's each and every person's right to dignity, a future bright.

These lofty ideals, they may claim, might not quite set their hearts aflame,
Rather, through their daily role when in support, or on patrol,
They aid and help their comrades there, to carry out their duties, where
Danger lurks and menace waits at every corner, door or gate,
And, nerves stretched taut at every turn, when omnipresent fear returns.

So are they heroes? That's to say, not in the more accepted way
Of glory hunting men of steel, dashing, wanting to appeal
To public gaze, be held in awe, strong silent guardians of the law.
These are average, common folk who like to laugh, enjoy a joke.
But if it's time to pay the price, they'll freely make that sacrifice.

For after all is said and done, to conquer fear and carry on,
Advancing into the unknown, even when all help is gone,
Is heroism beyond reproach, and we should honour those who touch
Our hearts by their example bright, who surely now, have earned the right
To stand among our heroes all, who boldly answered duty's call.

Passing Out Parade

The chairs lined up around the square, parents, siblings, girlfriends there,
Proudly wait expectantly for offspring to parade and see
The youngster who'd left home so green, to spread his wings,
   so eager, keen,
Mature into a fine young man, with back so straight, and fitter than
He'd ever been in days long past - a transformation, oh so vast!
They scarcely recognized the chap, immaculate, from toe to cap.

And as, so eagerly, they wait, a silence falls, then suddenly a great
Swell of sound invades the air, distantly, beyond the square.
Martial music, Pipes and Drums, diminished first, but nearer comes,
And growing louder with each beat, till the distant, marching feet,
In a perfect, synchronized ballet, appear, and smartly make their way
To take their stations, (oft rehearsed, on wintry mornings till well versed!)

The bands wheel left and take their post, playing till the boys, at last
Are then in place, by Company. And in the front, conspicuously,
Stand erect the senior men, no longer boys, and here again
Together for the last parade, as is their due. A farewell paid
By all who'll follow in their wake, examples of what they can make
Of their young lives while at the school, if they just observe the rules.

Inspection time, and while the Brass perambulate, and slowly pass
The tiered ranks, so smart, so still, the sound of music starts to fill
The air with haunting melodies, as Pipes and Drums perform, then cease
As Brass and Reed take up the role, quietly play to soothe the soul.
A lull, a pause in ceremony, time for the senior men, maybe,
To think a while on previous years,
   nostalgic thoughts, the laughs, the fears.

But now it all springs into life, the hoarse commands, sharp as a knife
Galvanise the waiting throng, as orders are obeyed as one.
The march past now, extended line, the bass drum beating in slow time,
As gleaming ranks pass by the dais. The "Eyes Right!" shout, and every face
Snaps round to proudly gaze upon the decorated chest of one
Whose rank entitles him to stand, saluting all, in manner grand.

/Then change to quick

71

Then change to quick time, arms now swing, pipes are skirling, chanters sing,
As ruler-straight ranks, heads held high, raise the dust as they march by.
White buckskin belts gleam in the sun, polished boots and buckles, shone
To burnished lustre bright, a truly great, impressive sight
That one won't easily forget, a really grand occasion, yet,
One that's tinged with sadness too, as men move on to pastures new.

And finally, the pass out starts, the bass drum throbs, and in the hearts
Of all who watch the closing scene, good fortune wished, as now between
The slowly closing gates they pass, symbolizing now at last,
The time they've spent here now is done, the next phase of their life begun.
And as they cheer, and caps fly high, their faces turned up to the sky,
In years to come, when in times thrall, this day they fondly will recall.

A Soldiers Tale (21st Century Style)

The soldier said, "I never thought," as he faced the seething throng,
"That the Pen was mightier than the Sword - I couldn't be more wrong!
I've got just five rounds in the mag, my body armour's duff,
My family lives in a slum, I think I've had enough!"

"That damned accountant, with his pen, up in the Treasury,
Is calculating where and when the next chop's going to be.
If he and all his cronies there had served Queen and Country,
He'd sure think twice and wouldn't dare to use that pen so free."

"They send us out - in harm's way, and haven't got a clue
What life is like, when day to day you know it could be YOU!
They have no understanding of the words by which we live,
'Loyalty', 'Truth', 'Comradeship', - Not 'Take, Take, Take' but 'Give'."

"From University they go, onto a stepping stone
To a sinecure, then a safe seat, no sweat, no effort? - NO!
Just a willingness to do as they are told, like sheep,
Rewards will surely then accrue, as up the scale they creep."

"And finally they reach the Top, the Ministries they prized,
Then at all costs, avoid the chop, as their worth is realized.
But self delusion has its day, reality no place,
They know they're right and others wrong,
Hard facts they will not face."

"Our troops have earned deserved renown, of that there is no doubt,
But useless Leaders let them down, and now they're getting out.
So don't expect things to improve, the country is in tatters,
But priorities are Balance Sheets and nought else really matters."

"So it all comes down to just one fact, that all things have a cost,
And while Accountants make the Rules,
                    HUMANITY IS LOST."

The only conquests which are permanent and leave no regrets, are our conquests over ourselves.

                                              Napolean Bonaparte

Regrets

I don't regret the day that I became a junior soldier,
I don't regret the lessons learned as I became much older.
I don't regret the knocks that I took in those bygone years,
I don't regret the bullying, the insults and the jeers.
I don't regret restrictive rules, which seemed so pointless then,
I don't regret months, cleaning kit, time and time again.
I don't regret the duties, when I'd sooner be at home,
I don't regret the years I served, the places that I've gone.
And, most of all, I don't regret loving the girl I married,
Who's stood by me through thick and thin, the children that she carried,
So tenderly and lovingly, through four score years and more,
Without complaint, when times were hard, the soul mate I adore.

But
I regret the time that's passed, and standards gone, which once we new.
I regret the passing of the friends I've known, faithful, good and true.
I regret some things I've said, without a thought of consequence.
I regret some of my deeds, when guaranteed to give offence.
I regret that now the world, in which we live, is so extreme.
I regret the innocence of childhood, disappearing, as a dream.
I regret the public figures, lying, grasping, without shame.
I regret distorted values and pursuit of transient fame.
But, most of all, my great regret is loss of freedom's choice
To exercise our innate right to stand erect, and voice
Opinions, sincerely held, free and without fear …..
But I regret that those good times will never reappear.

The 66'ers !

Of all the lads who, o'er the years, have passed through Boys' School's gates,
The sixty-six mob are front rank, for humour and strange tastes!
They're English, Irish, Welshmen, Scotsmen too, with even a Reverend,
Although I think that he'd keep quiet, about his choice of friends!

They need a fix of 'sossidges' to keep their spirits up,
And preferably, with a pint of hooch, though anything they'll sup.
As long as it's supplied for free they'll gladly swill it down
You have to see their capacity although it's probably grown

By constant practice in the mess o'er many, many years
And likely have reduced, I guess, many drunks to tears
By their sheer bloody staying power, while propping up the bar
These men are champions in their field, boozers, without par!

They're models of diversity, their interests manifold,
Post Office vans, and Chieftain tanks, and others, yet untold.
The trades they've followed, 'ECE's , Fitters, VM's 'A' and 'B',
With other various odds and sods, they've got variety!

Their twisted sense of humour, both irreverent and droll,
Keeps life's dark side from entering and twisting up the soul
Although I dare say, we all learned the same thing at young age
And it's another thing that binds us in our common heritage.

Yet this coin has another side, you'll not find better mates,
They'll stand together, side by side, and face what lies in wait
United, all, to stand or fall, as life's long battle's fought
Together, friends through thick and thin, they'll give each, full support.

So though they give the impression of a bunch of raving nuts,
Beneath the skin, they're just ex boys who'll always have the guts
To follow the examples set, in early days, long past,
To stand and fight for what is right, courageous and steadfast.

Discipline

Discipline's a funny thing - depends on how it's seen,
One persons view is counter to another's, and between
The two, their point of view can be somewhat obscure,
And one's abuse is seen by some as treatment that is fair.

By standards of the present day, as Jeeps we had it hard,
Being bullied and then bellowed at, it certainly appeared
That we would enter adulthood as psychological wrecks,
Yet, look around and it is clear that we survived intact.

Psychologists and theorists seem sometimes to ignore
The basic facts - that people are quite tough - and can endure
Much more than all the experts think, if they have got the will.
And human spirit can triumph and rise yet higher still.

But in this touchy feely world idealists reign supreme,
They say that all should win the race, no losers, it would seem
Should have to make the effort that's required to gain their goal,
Success should be obtained for free, to be enjoyed by all.

These are now the lessons that children are taught today,
No disappointments are allowed, no feelings hurt, no way
To feel responsible if others they upset,
It's not their fault, it's someone else to blame, no shame, regret.

But they are life's apprentices, and lessons should be learned,
That in a far from ideal world, rewards have to be earned,
And those who strive to make success, respecting others too,
Will greatly then enrich their lives, by all they say and do.

So ignore the politicians, and examples that they set,
The lying and the cheating, the thirst for power, and let
Integrity and Truth return, let realists, in time bring
Us to a Just and happier world, where common sense is King!

Whither Boys School?

There's a place just South of Reading,
in Berkshire's leafy lanes,
Where the builders ply their trade for all to see,
And the houses now are rising,
while the tractors and the cranes
Churn the ground beneath their wheels industriously.

In the midst of this chaotic scene, two pillars starkly wait,
Red brick, joined by an arch with torches there,
Proclaiming proudly of the boys who passed between their gates,
Into a life of comradeship and care.

They wait, on guard, like sentinels, as "progress" blunders in,
A barrier to hold the past in place,
Defending all the memories of things that once had been,
Against the march of time and mankind's race.
But nought will still the sands of time,
as through the glass they flow,
Their staunch defence may soon be overcome,
The symbols of our youth may vanish in the evening's glow,
A sacrifice to hunger for new homes.

The Garden, tended carefully, may soon be swept away,
The last remaining symbol of the past,
Replaced by flats and houses and children at play,
All evidence of past memories, laid to waste.

But memories can't be destroyed, as buildings surely can,
And Old Boys will remember constantly
The times when they were young, strong men,
fit to fight and fight again,
A band of brothers facing life, carefree.

And, years from now,
the residents may think they hear the noise
Of marching feet, or distant bugle blow,
The skirl of pipes,
the myriad sounds of thousands of young boys,
Who came to live those many years ago.

So, in this ever changing world,
when the past seems to have died,
The independent spirit does still thrive,
The vivid recollections still imbue the soul with pride
And "Boys' School" in its MEN will stay alive.

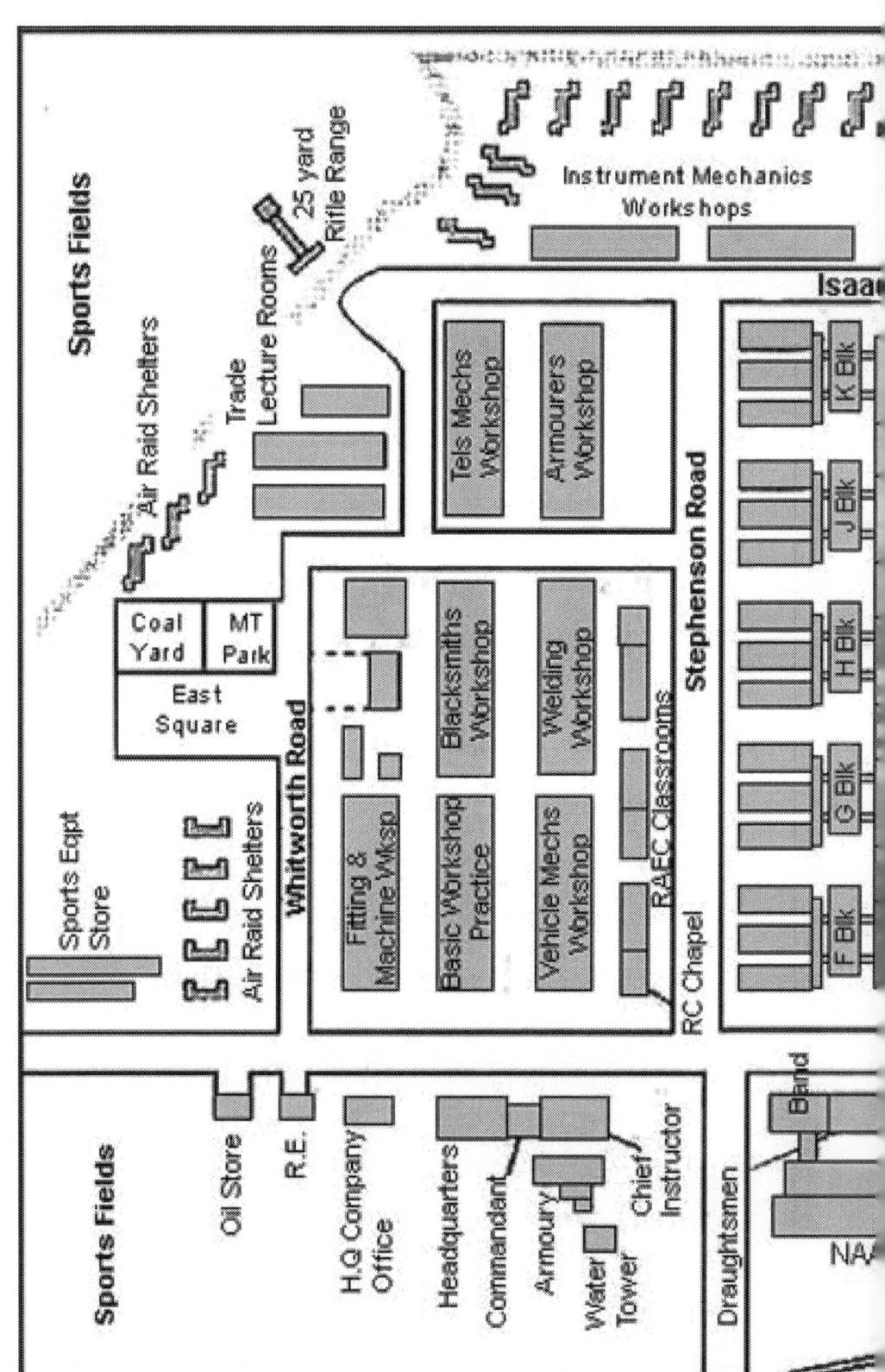

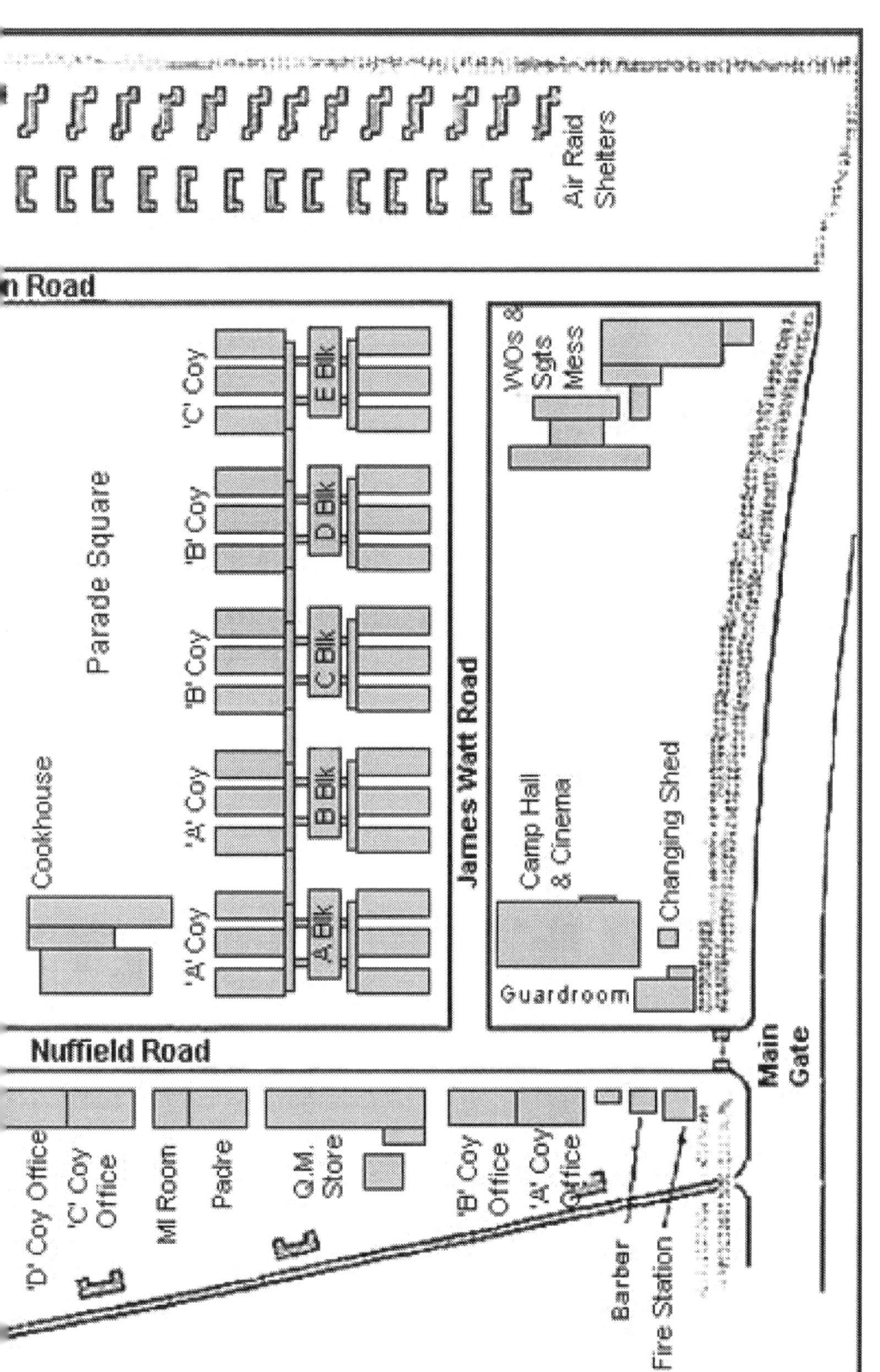

THE ENEMY WITHIN

From the craggy heights of Afghanistan down to Basra's dusty plains,
They serve with dogged steadfastness, Regiments, whose names
And ranks are being diluted by those who sent them there,
Small thanks for loyal service to the soldiers in their care.

They carry out their duties with discipline and nerve,
Despite indifferent masters who never had to serve
In uniform of any kind, who'll never comprehend
The qualities that go to make the worlds best fighting men.

These Ministers sit in Parliament in pampered luxury,
They're totally divorced - far from the grim reality
Of gut wrenching exhaustion, nerves taut, yet staying strong,
While calculating the price they'll pay, if they should get it wrong.

Not just the price of pain or death, which is a soldiers lot,
But predatory legal vultures, waiting for the shot
Which, in a stark, harsh courtroom, will implicate, incense,
A Soldier, in the heat of war, who fired in self defence.

Old soldiers, looking back at their times, serving overseas,
And fighting for their Country, possess great empathy
With serving troops today, who bear this burden, most unfair,
Scapegoats for political ends, in full publicity's glare.

How long before they cry, "Enough!" And finally walk away,
No blame could be attached to them, if ever came that day.
Yet this will never come about, the Army's proud tradition
Would never countenance defeat, whatever the position.

They will not bow to enemies, whether alien, or at home,
They'll press on with cast-iron resolve, until the battle's won.
And carry through to victory the fight they've undertaken,
Defeating all the hypocrites who've left them, unforsaken.

It comes to us, the Public, then, to give them full support,
And challenge all these Ministers to make every effort
To give them what is justly theirs, and honour all these men,
And fight, as they fight, valiantly, to gain justice for them.

The Glorious Past

Just a bare, sparse patch of ground,
A car park? Yes – but what's that sound?
The skirl of pipes, a bugle's call,
The tramp of feet, shouts mingle,
All around the ghosts are here,
Most young, fresh-faced, eyes eager, clear.

And other, older, stern of face,
All uniformed and with a grace
Of movement, a daily learned routine,
With heads held high, a polished sheen,
Reflecting out the morning sun,
The glorious past parades again.

A ghostly roll-call echoes on,
Names well-remembered, one by one.
McNally, Cook, Brady, Cole,
Sallies, Silvers, Huxley and all
Of those recalled from yesteryear,
Who earned respect (and sometimes fear!).

The memories, undimmed by time
Of tears and comradeship sublime,
Return again when we recall
How things once were, when we stood tall.
Prepared to face the future, proud,
To take on the world with heads unbowed.

So just a patch of ground? Maybe.
But it masks a long proud history
Of values gained, the will to strive,
Directions taken, the zest to live.
So if upon that ground you go,
And hear that ghostly bugle blow,
Remember all that once was there,
And, in remembrance, say a prayer.

For Old Comrades

If you're ill and feeling low,
Cheer up, because you'll always know
Your pals from way back will be there
To share the pain and maybe bear,
Or help to bear, life's onward toll,
And give support to those who fall
From fitness peak to depths unsung,
With lessons learned when we were young.
To help our friends to carry on,
Till all adversity is gone.
So hang on in there, force a grin,
You never were trained to give in
To setbacks great, or troubles small,
Your chums will rally, give their all
To help you back till you have won,
Stay with it, lad - you're not alone!

The Final Parade

He'll always be there, laughing, young and full of fun,
With all his pals around, true friends every one.
The things they've done together, bind them closer still,
Friendships born at tender age, endure, and always will.

Though life moves on, down well worn roads, and people come and go,
He'll cherish those whose time he shared, the ones he came to know
so well, when life was rich, the future still unread,
And boldly looking forward to the challenges ahead.

And through the intervening years, till mortal life's span ends,
He'll know that still, above all else, he had the gift of friends
who knew his faults, endearing ways, his strengths and foibles too,
As no one else could, in his time, workmates or colleagues new.

So at last, the Passing Out, when Goodbyes must be said,
He's reached his final goal, to join the pals who've gone ahead
to make a place for him, amongst all those on Heavens' Square,
Prepared to welcome those who come, their comradeship to share.

Outsiders never understand the bond that holds us tight,
It's difficult to put in words, it's like a shining light
that guides us through life's tortuous path until the final end,
But sums it up in six small words - "He was my Pal, my Friend."

1970 Recruiting Poster

Young TeeCee

www.ingramcontent.com/pod-product-compliance
Ingram Content Group UK Ltd.
Pitfield, Milton Keynes, MK11 3LW, UK
UKHW041451180426
11946UKWH00013B/151/J